AF486252

i

CHRISTIAN BIBLE DRAMA SERIES

Christmas Edition

A DREAM COME TRUE

From the first Creation to the new creation and from the prophets to the Christ

A Christmas musical/pageant based on the creation of humankind, our fall into sin and the inevitable coming of the Messiah to take us out of sin

A presentation with music, drama, poetry and dance all interwoven into one continuous narrative

REV. DR. ERROL E. LESLIE

Copyright © 2024 **Errol Leslie Publishing**

Published in the United States of America

ISBN 979-8-89395-869-0 (SC)

Errol Leslie Publishing

222 West 6th Street
Suite 400, San Pedro, CA, 90731
errollesliepublishing@gmail.com
321 614 1456

Order Information and Rights Permission:

Quantity sales. Special discounts might be available on quantity purchases by corporations, associations, and others. For details, contact the publisher at the address above.

For Book Rights Adaptation and other Rights Permission.
Call us at toll-free 1-888-945-8513 or send us an email at admin@stellarliterary.com.

I was blessed to be part of a theatrical production many years ago that brought together young people for an ecumenical ministry in the arts. I made lifelong friends, found a place to belong, and explored the limits, as well as leanings of my creative gifts. It was as a result of the lifelong creative foresight, insight, and genius of the Rev. Dr. Errol Leslie to whom I am forever indebted for the opportunity to play the character Lois. I reflect with fondness on the richness of the experience; it will always be held up as one of the best times in my youth when my skills and mind as a young person were affirmed and encouraged. We thank God for Rev. Leslie and trust that his example will be a template for youth ministry leaders.

—Candice Walker

Attorney-at-law, Kingston, Jamaica

This magnificent production brought to life an energetic reality of the Christmas story. Being a part of it was not only an honor, but the memory and excitement has left an indelible mark on all of us. As a very young pastor at the time, Rev. Leslie outdid himself by scripting, directing, and overseeing a successful play that left the audience very inspired.

—Nigel Reynolds

Dallas, Texas

It was an honor to have played Mary during the inaugural production in 1985. The memories of the energy, pride, and excitement still linger on. Our writer, director, producer, Rev. Leslie, masterfully combined his roles to ensure we delivered at every performance.

—Melissa Gooden-Bowleg

Nassau, Bahamas

I was thrilled to perform as Mary in one of Reverend Leslie's well-received, Christian theatrical productions.

—Simone Clarke

Florida, USA

Following is an official OnlineBookClub.org review of "Christian Bible Drama Series -" by Rev Dr. Errol E. Leslie.] *5 out of 5 stars*

Rev. Dr. Errol E. Leslie creates two storylines that portray the events leading up to the birth of the Lord Jesus Christ in his book, ***Christian Bible Drama Series, Christmas Edition.*** This book is a collection of two dramas with the same message: the birth of Jesus Christ. Despite the differences in the storylines of both stories, certain key characters and events remain constant, such as the villainous character of King Herod and the saving power of God.

The stories involve the divine conception of a poor young girl, Mary, who was, at the time, betrothed to a young carpenter named Joseph. She gets that this may affect her engagement with him, but with the help of an angel, Joseph still takes her as his wife. When they eventually give birth to the child, King Herod does everything within his power to see that the ancient prophecy about the child does not come to pass.

Leslie uses this book to teach about the origin of Christmas and the importance of the celebration of Christmas in the Christian faith. The book has a touch of humor. For example, in the first story, despite the depletion of gold in Herod's country, the three wise men he sent to visit baby Jesus took gold to give him as one of the presents.

There are certain positive aspects of the book. First, the book is written in a simple and understandable language. Second, the author uses the book to teach certain lessons to Christians. For example, the author taught that God will not allow a person to be in a situation that the person cannot handle. This is exemplified in the story involving Mary when she was afraid of how Joseph would react to the news of her pregnancy. The book also teaches that God will certainly do everything to guide His own.

Despite King Herod's decree for the killing of male children under the age of two, God still saved baby Jesus. Another positive aspect of the book is that it contains songs that can be sung independently during Christmas, and the author also provides the sol-fa notations of some songs.

I only found one error in the book. This shows that the book was professionally edited. Added to the positives identified above, I will be giving the book five out of five stars. The negative aspect I found was insufficient to deduct a star from my rating. I recommend this book to all Christians, especially those interested in Christmas dramas.

Book To Film Review

The Christmas Journey" is a spectacular and emotionally resonant cinematic adaptation of the book "Christian Bible Drama Series, Christmas Edition (Revised Edition)." This captivating film brings to life the untold details and deep emotions surrounding the Christmas story, offering a fresh and visually stunning perspective on this beloved narrative.

Set in the ancient world, "The Christmas Journey" takes audiences on a breathtaking and immersive adventure through the lives of Joseph, Mary, and the other key characters of the Christmas narrative. The film explores the doubts, challenges, and profound faith that shaped their journey, while also delving into the societal pressures, gossip, and rumors that surrounded them.

Through meticulous attention to historical accuracy and awe-inspiring visual effects, "The Christmas Journey" transports viewers to the bustling streets of Bethlehem, the majestic halls of Herod's palace, and the serene beauty of the Judean countryside. The film's stunning cinematography and intricate set designs create a visually mesmerizing experience that truly brings the ancient world to life.

At the heart of "The Christmas Journey" are its powerful musical numbers. From soul-stirring solos to breathtaking ensemble performances, the film's original songs and choreography elevate the storytelling to new heights. Each musical moment serves as a window into the characters' innermost thoughts and emotions, allowing the audience to connect deeply with their journey and experiences.

As the story unfolds, "The Christmas Journey" emphasizes the universal themes of love, hope, and redemption. It showcases the transformative power of faith and the profound impact that a single act of obedience can have on the world. Through its engaging narrative and heartfelt performances, the film invites viewers to reflect on the true meaning of Christmas and the enduring message of peace and goodwill.

"The Christmas Journey" is a cinematic experience that will captivate audiences of all ages, believers and non-believers alike. It celebrates the beauty of the Christmas story while offering a fresh perspective that resonates with modern audiences. This visually stunning and emotionally resonant film is destined to become a beloved holiday classic, reminding us all of the power of faith, love, and the Christmas spirit.

Review from Explora books

Synopsis:

"Christian Bible Drama Series, Christmas Edition" takes readers on an extraordinary journey, diving deep into the untold emotions and unexplored details of the beloved Christmas narrative. Weaving together poetry, drama, music, and dance, the book breathes new life into the characters and events of that transformative season. It delves into the doubts, conflicts, and human experiences that surrounded the birth of Jesus, capturing the hearts and imaginations of readers.

The musical creates a visually captivating and emotionally resonant adaptation that will engage and inspire audiences worldwide. It holds immense potential to captivate audiences and leave a lasting impact. It will transport viewers into the vibrant scenes, immerse them in the characters' emotions, and allow them to experience the Christmas story in a profoundly personal way. The added visual and auditory elements will deepen the connection between the audience and the narrative, making it a truly transformative and memorable experience.

Highlights:

The musical has emotional depth as it brings to life the raw human emotions and conflicts faced by characters like Joseph and Mary, offering a fresh and relatable perspective on their journey. Audiences will witness their doubts, struggles, and unwavering faith, forging a profound connection with the story.

Imaginative retelling: It incorporates imaginative scenes and interwoven elements which breathes new life into the Christmas story, offering a unique and captivating take on its timeless themes. This creative approach will engage audiences and spark their curiosity, inviting them to reflect on the narrative in fresh and thought-provoking ways.

EXPLORA BOOKS, BOOK REVIEW-TWO

"Christian Bible Drama Series, Christmas Edition" is an exceptional literary work that beautifully reimagines the timeless tale of the Christmas narrative. Pastor Leslie's revised edition takes readers on a captivating journey, exploring the untold emotions, conflicts, and intricate details surrounding the birth of Jesus. Through a masterful blend of poetry, drama, music, and dance, the author breathes new life into familiar characters and events, leaving readers spellbound.

What sets this book apart is its ability to evoke a deep sense of empathy and connection with the characters. Pastor Leslie artfully delves into the inner thoughts and struggles of figures like Joseph and Mary, inviting readers to experience their doubts, fears, and unwavering faith. By peeling back the layers of these characters' humanity, the author unveils a profound and relatable narrative that resonates with readers on a personal level.

The imaginative retelling of the Christmas story is nothing short of captivating. The inclusion of imaginative scenes and interwoven elements adds richness and depth to the familiar plot, sparking curiosity and challenging readers to contemplate the untold aspects of this transformative season. The author's vivid descriptions and meticulous attention to detail create a vivid tapestry that transports readers to the heart of biblical times.

Rating: ★★★★★ (5/5)

"Christian Bible Drama Series, Christmas Edition" is a literary masterpiece that deserves the highest praise. Pastor Leslie's work is a testament to the enduring power of storytelling, and this book is a must-read for anyone seeking a fresh and evocative retelling of the Christmas story.

"Christian Bible Drama Series, Christmas Edition," will touch the hearts of audiences, igniting a renewed sense of faith and hope. By staying true to the underlying theme of evangelism, the adaptation will encourage viewers to believe in Jesus and embrace the transformative power of His love.

CONTENTS

FOREWORD

When I was in seventh or eighth grade at school, I happened to have gone past the room which was used then as the school's auditorium following school one evening. In that room, there was a group of older students who were rehearsing what turned out to be a play. I was so intrigued by what was going on that I watched the proceedings from outside for about half an hour. Sometime on the following day, I inquired and sought some specifics as to what was really happening, and I was told that it was the school's drama group preparing for the annual secondary school's drama festival I then asked if I could be a part of the group and was told that I was late for that year, but I could try for the following year. Interestingly, I also noticed that there was at least one student in the group who was younger than I was, so I felt kind of jealous.

I realized that I had had a natural passion for drama as I basically counted down the days for the next season and enthusiastically attended the first audition for parts to be given out for the play which was going to be done that following year. I was not totally disappointed because I was given a part as an understudy for one character. From that time forth, I was a part of the school's drama group and participated in every major production until I graduated. I enjoyed it immensely, and before I knew it, I was playing major star roles in my high school's drama productions. For this introduction to theater, I recognize and pay tribute to my late high school vice principal who eventually became principal, Mr. Gordon Mead. While he is no longer with us, I would also acknowledge that his son, Andrew, remains in touch with his schoolmates through Facebook. Andrew was a very talented actor and, I might add, a natural comedian. God bless you, Andrew.

I also remember Mr. Roderick Ebanks and Ms. Karen Traynor as theater/drama teachers. While I do not know the life status of the latter two, I will note that they were both very supportive and helped to develop my early interest.

As far as schoolmates are concerned, I also acknowledge and recognize Mr. Basil Dawkins who eventually became a professional playwright and producer. I remember inviting Basil to attend a live performance of one of these musicals in 1989. He and I and a few other persons were engaged in an informal chit-chat following the production. In giving his feedback on the play, he said "This is one of the best Christmas plays that I have ever seen, and I have seen many." Basil, those words still resonate, and thirty-six years later, I still feel encouraged by those comments.

I also acknowledge the immediate former administrator general of Jamaica, Ms. Lona Brown. She was not only my classmate, but we co-starred in several high school productions in the early seventies. I remember very well seeing her perform in that first play which rehearsal I watched and was also moved by and impressed with her theater skills.

In twelfth grade (sixth form), as I battled with Shakespeare, Lord Byron, Chaucer, Jane Austen, Aldous Huxley, et al., in English Literature, I was again fortunate to have the above-mentioned Mrs. Lona Brown, as well as Mr. Glenroy Mellish, Mr. Henry Wright, and several others as my classmates sitting at the feet of Mr. Watts learning how to analyze poems, plays, and other pieces of literature.

Some fundamentals about writing would have stuck with me from my interaction with those classmates and teachers.

Once I graduated high school, I taught as a pretrained teacher at a secondary school. I immediately started a drama and music club, and in the one year I was there, I was able to get the students to put on an original play which I had written for a concert and which also included some music and singing.

I continued pursuing my innate passion for the arts when I entered seminary at the United Theological College of the West Indies, and for four years, I was part of both the drama group as well as the UTCWI Singers.

There was a parallel situation developing while I explored music and drama at the levels mentioned. I was also leader for my church's youth group, and I was constantly writing, directing, and producing short plays. Several of these plays were done at a competitive level while others were just done causally in church but would always carry a message. Several of the short plays which I wrote then were performed in a few neighboring churches.

In the year 1980, I had already graduated seminary and was working in the Manchester Circuit of Methodist Churches in Jamaica. One of the congregations would have an annual Christmas play, and I watched the plays for the first two years. As I watched the performance the second year, it occurred to me that while those performances have the message, they lacked creativity and intrigue.

I thought that we could do productions at a higher standard and with a little more substance. So early in the year 1982, I began writing the first of my two Christmas musicals: ***A Dream Come True.***

The young people across the circuit embraced it, and during the Christmas season of that year, we performed it about twelve times in different towns across Central Jamaica. It was really well received, and I gave thought at that time to publishing the script for that play.

A number of factors, including financial constraints, prevented me from publishing it at the time, so I basically just secured the script with the thought that I would publish it later.

Well, "later" has just arrived and so..........

Finally, after almost forty years since it was written, I offer this Christmas musical to the world. I trust that it will be found to be uplifting and the intended message of Christmas will resonate with persons across the world.

More importantly, I pray that lives will be changed spiritually and for the better as a result of whether watching these productions being done or participating in them in one way or the other.

PREFACE

This Christmas musical can be used in any one of several ways. It can be used in it's entirety as a full-length production or specific scenes can be extracted from it and shared as shorter plays. Depending on the setting, there are instances where the music or songs may be omitted although doing so may take away from the flow of the plot. As such, I would encourage directors to include the music and the dance, as these combinations certainly do add to the effect of the message. Directors may have a part of the cast sing the group songs, but it might be just as or even more effective if there was a separate choir and maybe orchestra preparing and singing the group musical pieces at the appropriate time.

Where appropriate, the original songs may even be recited as poems in certain settings. This musical was originally written for youth and young adults to share in during the season of advent.

However, if there is an opportunity for more senior adults to participate, they would be welcomed to do so. Where appropriate, players are encouraged to direct some statements to the audience since the hope is that the Christmas message would resonate again with persons in the audience.

Thank you for your interest in this Christmas musical and with your prayers and God's help, I trust that there will be several more musicals flowing from my pen which would be centered around biblical stories and plots. This one is from the Christmas edition, but hopefully, there will be more to come.

Hence the general title of this series, **Christian Drama Bible Series**.

A DREAM COME TRUE

A Christmas musical/pageant based on the creation of humankind, our fall into sin, and the inevitable coming of the Messiah to take us out of sin.

Written by Errol E. Leslie

Characters:

Herod: The king

Tamar: His wife

Perez: Herod's first attendant Azor: Herod's second attendant

Obed: Herod's third attendant

Asa: Herod's fourth attendant

Luke (young)

Luke (grown up)

Martha: Luke's wife

Virginia: Luke's sister

Susanna: Luke's mother

Mary: A young lady in the community

Joseph: A young man in the community

Mark: Joseph's first younger brother Aaron:

Joseph's second younger brother

Sarah: A God-fearing woman

David: A God-fearing man

Prophets

Amos, Hosea, Isaiah

Dancers

Singers

Readers

Prologue

An empty stage—Darkness Instrumental version of "It Came upon a Midnight Clear" or other appropriate Christmas carol is played. (*Offstage*)

Narrator/Voice   (*soft background music*) Before the world came into being, there was nothing…

Well, there was darkness, disorder, chaos, and confusion…and there was a Supreme Being, a Great Force, a Mighty Fortress, a Powerful Hand that said, "Let there be light."

(*All the lights are tuned on and off again after 10 seconds. Dancers come on for a dance during darkness. Stage lights come on, then dance to song "And the Lord Said Let There Be Light" or other appropriate song related to God's creation of light—dancers leave stage*)

Narrator/Voice   And so, it was in the beginning, God created the heaven and the earth; He also made light. And the light shone over all the earth. God made man (*Man appears on stage) and woman (Woman appears on stage)*

And from man and woman came their offspring (*More persons come on stage*) God made the waters (*Demonstrated by pictures on screen or replica on stage*)

The birds of the air (*demonstrated by pictures on screen or replica on stage*)

The fishes in the sea, (*Demonstrated by pictures on screen or replica on stage*)

The animals (*Demonstrated by pictures on screen or replica on stage*) Mountains and hills and rivers. God made the fruit trees that provided food for mankind. Then God looked at all that He had made and said, "That's good! That's really good." Then man looked at all that God had made and man fell down and worshipped God.

(*Players turn around, back to audience; kneel and point to painting on screen depicting the creation.*)

Narrator/Voice   Their mouths continually spoke of the goodness of
                            the Lord.

(*Choral/verse speaking by group: Psalm 148*)

Psalm 148

Praise the Lord. Praise the Lord from the heavens; praise him in the heights above.

Praise him, all his angels; praise him, all his heavenly hosts. Praise him, sun and moon; praise him, all you shining stars. Praise him, you highest heavens and you waters above the skies.

Let them praise the name of the Lord, for at his command they were created, and he established them for ever and ever—he issued a decree that will never pass away.

Praise the Lord from the earth, you great sea creatures and all ocean depths, lightning and hail, snow and clouds, stormy winds that do his bidding, you mountains and all hills; fruit trees and all cedars, wild animals and all cattle, small creatures and flying birds, kings of the earth and all nations, you princes and all rulers on earth, young men and women, old men and children.

Let them praise the name of the Lord, for his name alone is exalted; his splendor is above the earth and the heavens.

And he has raised up for his people a horn, the praise of all his faithful servants, of Israel, the people close to his heart.

Praise the Lord

Narrator/Voice	And there was a woman whose name was Sarah. She feared the Lord and loved Him. And there was also a man. His name was David. (*They appear respectively on stage as they are introduced.*)
Sarah	Oh, David, what shall we do? God has been so good to us.
David	I shall sing of the mercies of the Lord forever. His praise shall continually be in my mouth.
Sarah	We will have to be obedient to His laws and statutes.
David	We shall have to offer sacrifices. O come let us worship and fall down and kneel before the Lord our maker. For He is the Lord our God, and we are the people of His Pasture and the Sheep of His Hand.
Sarah	Let us make a temple to be used for the worship of our Lord, and whosoever shall enter into the gates of this temple, let them do so with thanksgiving.
David	Look at the mountains and hills (*Points to painting or other depiction of the mountains*) Look at the rivers and trees, the sun and moon and the stars. Look at all his peoples. (*Points to painting*) All things created by the hands of the Lord.
Sarah	(*Approaches downstage to audience*) All things bright and beautiful All creatures great and small

All things wise and wonderful The Lord God made them all.

David   (*also goes downstage to audience*) Great is the Lord, and greatly to be praised, in the city of our God, in the mountain of His Holiness. O, Sarah, come let us sing unto the Lord, let us heartily rejoice in the strength of our Salvation. Let us sing unto the Lord a new song for He has done marvelous things.

Sarah   Make a joyful noise unto God, all ye lands; sing forth the honor of His name; make His name glorious. Come and hear all ye that fear God and I will declare what he hath done for my soul (*Sarah sings aloud the first verse of the hymn "How Great Thou Art." Other players join her on stage as all join in singing the chorus "Then Sings My Soul."*)

Narrator/Voice   And as they recognized more and more their dependence on God, they continued to acknowledge His goodness. He provided them with everything in time of need and protected them in time of danger. They had everything and lacked nothing and about this they were bold to speak.

(*Choral speaking: Psalm 23*)

The Lord is my shepherd, I lack nothing. He makes me lie down in green pastures, he leads me beside quiet waters, he refreshes my soul. He guides me along the right paths for his name's sake.

Even though I walk through the darkest valley, I will fear no evil, for you are with me; your rod and your staff, they comfort me. You prepare a table before me in the presence of my enemies. You anoint my head with oil; my cup overflows. Surely your goodness and love will follow me all the days of my life, and I will dwell in the house of the Lord forever.

Narrator/Voice   That was their promise, but did they really dwell
                               their forever? No! They strayed from Him. God's
                               own people whom He had made and who sang
                               forth His praises now turned their backs upon
                               Him, and before long, they had become a
                               rebellious people and were involved in all kinds of
                               sin.

They turned from the true God and worshipped false gods, pagan gods, graven images.

(*Demonstrated by pictures on screen or replica on stage*)

They were involved in sexual immorality, adultery, and possessed a lustful eye.

(*Two or three couples walk onstage depicting love affairs*)

There was great oppression as the rich got richer and the poor became poorer. They sold the righteous for silver and the needy for a pair of sandals. They trampled on the heads of the poor as upon the dust of the ground. They denied justice to the oppressed. The poor were cheated and always subject to oppression.

(*Demonstrated by pictures/video on screen or replica on stage*)

There was great drunkenness. All over Israel, there was immorality, dishonesty, stealing, lying, killing, and blasphemy. And all their work displeased the Lord, and he regretted that He had made man. For man was created in the image of God as perfect beings. The Lord saw how great man's wickedness on earth was and that all the inclination of the thoughts of his heart was only evil all the time. The Lord was grieved that He had made man on earth and His heart was filled with pain. So the Lord said, "I will wipe mankind whom I have created from the face of the earth—men, animals, and creatures that move along the ground, and birds of the air for I am grieved that I have made them."

And in sorrow the people sang…

Rev. Dr. Errol E. Leslie
THE LORD, HE MADE US

The Lord, he made us, He made us good
The Lord, he gave us, He gave us food
Be fruitful and multiply, and glorify and magnify
The Lord who made us all must be deified

CHO

A Prophet from The Lord will come upon the earth A prophet, priest, and king will soon be given birth To save the wicked people, from sorrow, fear and sin So, all who call upon His name will enter in.

Then Satan entered, he entered man
He said Just do wrong; do all you can:
Just be at ease, do as you please and always cease to keep the peace
Release the rules and that way your joy will increase

O Lord, we humbly confess to you
That we have done wrong; we've messed up too
So please forgive that we may live and then receive and not deceive
Together we will serve so you won't be peeved

Now let us raise up our hands and sing
All glory and praises to the new born King
We glorify and magnify and deify as we go by
We thank and honor Him whose love is always nigh

Narrator/Voice	And so, with a great anxiety the people waited for their Prophet. But who was he to be? Where was he to come from? For many prophets did come, but no one knew who was the greatest of them. One prophet came from Tekoa, south of Israel.

He did not think that there was much hope for Israel and prophesied doom for all the people… And his name was Amos.

(The following statements by the three prophets may or may not have background accompanying music)

Amos

The Lord roars from Zion and thunders from Jerusalem, the pastures of the Shepherds dry up and the top of the camel withers. For three sins of Damascus, even for four, I will not turn back my wrath. For three sins of Gaza or Tyre of Edom or Ammon or Moab or Judah, even for four, I will not turn back my wrath. Because they have rejected the Day of the Lord and have not kept his decrees, because they have been led astray by false gods, the gods their ancestors followed. I will send fire upon Judah that will consume the fortresses of Jerusalem. You only have I chosen of all the families of the earth; therefore, I will punish you for all your sins. Hear this, you cows of Bashan on Samaria. You women who oppress the poor and crush the needy and say to your husbands, "Bring us some drinks," the time will surely come when you will be taken away with hooks; you will be cast out toward Mt. Harmon. Seek good, not evil that you may live. Then the Lord Almighty will be with you. Hate evil, love good, and maintain justice in the courts, or there will be wailing in all the streets and cries of anguish in every public square. Woe to you who long for the day of the Lord. That will be darkness, not light. I will send you into exile beyond Damascus says the Lord whose name is God Almighty.

Narrator/Voice

And from the North came another whose name was Hosea.

Hosea

Hear the word of the Lord, you Israelites, because the Lord has a charge to bring against you who live in the land. There is no faithfulness, no love, no acknowledgement of God in the land. There is only cursing, lying and murder, stealing, adultery; they break all bounds and bloodsheds follow bloodsheds... But let no man bring a charge. Let no man accuse another for your people are like those who bring charges against a priest.

Come let us return to the Lord. He has torn us to pieces, but He will heal us.
He has injured us, but He will bind up our wounds. After two days, he will revive us. On the third day, He will restore us that we may live in His presence. Return, O Israel, to the Lord your God. Your sins have been your downfall! Take words with you and return to the Lord. The ways of the Lord are right; the righteous walk in them, but the rebellious stumble in them.

Narrator/Voice

And from the lips of Isaiah came these words.

Isaiah

The spirit of the Lord is upon me because the Lord hath anointed me to preach good things unto the meek. He hath sent me to bind up the captives, and the opening of the prison to them that are bound; to proclaim the acceptable year of the Lord and the day of our God, to comfort those who mourn and provide for those who grieve in Zion.

Here is my servant whom I uphold my chosen one in whom I delight, I will put my spirit upon Him and He will bring justice to the nations. He will not shout or cry out or raise His voice in the streets. In faithfulness He will bring forth justice; He will not falter or be discouraged

until He establishes justice on earth. In His law, the islands will put their hope.

I the Lord called you in righteousness, I will take hold of your hand.

I will keep you and will make you to be a covenant for the people and a light for the Gentiles. To open eyes that are blind to free captives from prison and to release from the dungeon those who sit in darkness.

Hast thou not seen, hast thou not heard that the Lord is the everlasting God, the Creator of the ends of the earth. He will not grow tired or weary and his understanding no one can fathom. He gives strength to the weary and increase the power of the weak. Even youths grow tired and weary and young men stumble and fall, but those who hope in the Lord will renew their strength, they shall soar on wings like eagles, they will run and not grow weary, they shall walk and not faint. So do not fear for I am with you; do not be dismayed, for I am your God. I will strengthen you and help you. I will uphold you with my righteous hand. The Lord himself will give you a sign. A virgin will be with child and will give birth to a son and will call him Immanuel. He will eat curds and honey when he knows enough to reject the wrong and choose the right.

The people walking in darkness have seen a great light; on those living in the land of the shadows of death, a light has dawned. You have enlarged the nation and increased their joy.

They rejoice before you as people rejoice at the harvest, as men rejoice when dividing the plunder. For as in the day of Midian's defeat,

Rev. Dr. Errol E. Leslie

you have shattered the yoke that burdens them, the bar across their shoulders, the rod of their oppressor.

Every warrior's boot used in battle and every garment rolled in blood will be destined for burning, will be fuel for fire. For unto us a child is born; to us a son is given and the government will be on His shoulders.

(Background music: song "For Unto Us a Child Is Born" is played live or prerecorded during which dancers appear on stage and perform.

During music, Isaiah continues to mime message. At the end of the dance, a little boy enters at side stage. His name is Luke

ACT I, SCENE 1
The Streets of Nazareth

Luke	Sir, what is this news I hear? What message is it that you are proclaiming?
Isaiah	The birth of a king; a child is to be born, and He will be King.
Luke	A child made king? A child like me? But we already have a king. Herod is the—
Isaiah	Herod is an earthly king. I speak of a heavenly King; a descendant of David who shall rule the whole world. He will be called wonderful Counselor, Mighty God, Everlasting Father, Prince of Peace. Of the increase of His government and peace, there will be no end. He will reign on David's throne and over His Kingdom, establishing and upholding it with justice and righteousness from that time on and forever.
Luke	This is certainly some news. If a child is made king, then it means that children will be regarded highly in this country, and that's just what I would want. I would be one of His armor-bearers; I

Rev. Dr. Errol E. Leslie

would be one of his followers and among His chosen friends. But…how would Herod take this?

Isaiah   In his own time, he will call all men unto himself, even those who have strayed from *God (and then sarcastically)* How will Herod take this? How will Herod take this? (*Confidently*) Even Herod will have to bow before Him. He has sinned no less than all others. Look at all God's people. (*Pointing at the audience*) They were all born in sin and shaped in iniquity… And Herod is one of them. They must all bow down and worship Him as soon as He is born.

Luke   Yes, I remember my mother telling me… She told me how God had made us all in His own image as perfect beings and that our forefathers used to praise God in the wilderness and even down in Egypt. But afterward, men became sinful and disobedient. They turned away from the true God and worshipped false gods.

Isaiah   And this situation continues even until now. We all like sheep have gone astray, each of us has turned to his own way.

Luke   But what has this got to do with the King coming?

Isaiah   Because mankind has been sinful and has turned away from God, God has sent this King who will draw men back to Him. His coming will bring joy and peace into the world because He will reconcile man to God. For those who have sinned, He would take the punishment. That's why He is coming. Hear now the voice of God! Let the people of God… Let the remnant of Israel shout the message. It is there for all to hear.

(*Choral/Verse Speaking: Isaiah 53*)

Who has believed our message and to whom has the arm of the Lord been revealed? He grew up before him like a tender shoot, and like a root out of dry ground.

He had no beauty or majesty to attract us to him, nothing in his appearance that we should desire him.

He was despised and rejected by mankind, a man of suffering, and familiar with pain.

Like one from whom people hide their faces he was despised, and we held him in low esteem.

Surely, he took up our pain and bore our suffering, yet we considered him punished by God, stricken by him, and afflicted.

But he was pierced for our transgressions, he was crushed for our iniquities; the punishment that brought us peace was on him, and by his wounds we are healed.

We all, like sheep, have gone astray, each of us has turned to our own way;

and the Lord has laid on him the iniquity of us all.

He was oppressed and afflicted, yet he did not open his mouth; he was led like a lamb to the slaughter, and as a sheep before its shearers is silent, so he did not open his mouth.

By oppression and judgment, he was taken away. Yet who of his generation protested? For he was cut off from the land of the living; for the transgression of my people, he was punished.

He was assigned a grave with the wicked, and with the rich in his death, though he had done no violence, nor was any deceit in his mouth. Yet it was the Lord's will to crush him and cause him to suffer, and though the Lord makes his life an offering for sin, he will see his offspring and prolong his days, and the will of the Lord will prosper in his hand.

After he has suffered, he will see the light of life and be satisfied; by his knowledge, my righteous servant will justify many,

And he will bear their iniquities and intercession for the transgressors.

"Group leaves stage"

Isaiah

I must be gone too. I must go with the people of God. We have to continue with the proclamation of the message. You should… indeed, you must be a messenger too. Go sing of the King who is coming to reign. Bear the news to every land; go spread the joyful news. Go pray for your sins, because the sins of your parents have become your sins. (*Shouts to group leaving stage*) Hey, wait for me! Wait! Wait!

Luke

(*to himself*) The sins of my parents have become my sins? Go pray for my sins…so I have sinned too. (*On his knees in sudden exclamation*) Have mercy on me, O God, according to your unfailing love; according to your great compassion blot out my transgressions. Wash away all my iniquity and cleanse me from my sin. For I know my transgressions, and my sin is always before me. Against you, you only, have I sinned and done what is evil in your sight; so you are right in your verdict and justified when you judge. Surely, I was sinful at birth, sinful from the time my mother conceived me. Yet you desired faithfulness even in the womb; you taught me wisdom in that secret place. Cleanse me with hyssop, and I will be clean; wash me, and I will be whiter than snow. Let me hear joy and gladness; let the bones you have crushed rejoice. Hide your face from my sins and blot out all my iniquity. Create in me a pure heart, O God, and renew a steadfast spirit within me. Do not cast me from your presence or take your Holy Spirit from me. Restore to me the joy of your salvation and grant me a willing spirit, to sustain me. Then I will teach transgressors your ways, so that sinners will turn back to you.

> Deliver me from the guilt of bloodshed, O God, you who are God my Savior, and my tongue will sing of your righteousness. Open my lips, Lord, and my mouth will declare your praise. You do not delight in sacrifice, or I would bring it; you do not take pleasure in burnt offerings. My sacrifice, O God, is a broken spirit; a broken and contrite heart you, God, will not despise.

(Psalm 103: choral/verse speaking)

Bless the Lord, O my soul; And all that is within me, bless His holy name!
Bless the Lord, O my soul, And forget not all His benefits:
Who forgives all your iniquities, Who heals all your diseases,
Who redeems your life from destruction, Who crowns you with lovingkindness and tender mercies,
Who satisfies your mouth with good things, So that your youth is renewed like the eagle's.
The Lord executes righteousness And justice for all who are oppressed.
He made known His ways to Moses, His acts to the children of Israel. The Lord is merciful and gracious, Slow to anger, and abounding in mercy.
He will not always strive with us, Nor will He keep His anger forever. He has not dealt with us according to our sins, Nor punished us according to our iniquities.
For as the heavens are high above the earth, So great is His mercy toward those who fear Him;
As far as the east is from the west, So far has He removed our transgressions from us.
As a father pities his children, So the Lord pities those who fear Him. For He [a]knows our frame; He remembers that we are dust.
As for man, his days are like grass; As a flower of the field, so he flourishes.
For the wind passes over it, and it is gone, And its place remembers it no more.
But the mercy of the Lord is from everlasting to everlasting

On those who fear Him, And His righteousness to children's children, To such as keep His covenant, And to those who remember His commandments to do them.

The Lord has established His throne in heaven, And His kingdom rules over all.

Bless the Lord, you His angels, Who excel in strength, who do His word, Heeding the voice of His word.

Bless the Lord, all you His hosts, You ministers of His, who do His pleasure.

Bless the Lord, all His works, In all places of His dominion. Bless the Lord, O my soul!

Luke	*(Luke rises from his knees and continues confidently.)* Yes, I believe it; a child will be born and He will be made King. I have that dream. I have a dream that God will become man and one day reconcile the world to Himself. I have a dream that one is coming to save His people from their sins. I want Him to come now! I want Him to come now!
	(Sings solo "Come Thou Long Expected Jesus Born to Set Thy People Free." As he leaves the stage, the other players come on singing
	"Sing We The King Who Is Coming to Reign,"
	Then curtain.)

ACT I, SCENE 2
The palace of Herod

It is approaching entertainment time for the king. With the king are four attendants. They are Obed, Asa, Perez, and Azor. Tamar, the wife of Herod, is not yet in the company. They are discussing national affairs.

Herod	The supply of gold continues to dwindle, and soon, the coffers will be empty.
Asa	Well, what do we do to stop the decline, Your Majesty?
Obed	Do we have anything else for export or even exchange?
Herod	I say again, we shall have to sell men as slaves.
Asa	Make the decree, sir.
Herod	The decree is made. We shall begin with the older men. The word shall be out in the morrow.
Asa	It shall go out, Your Majesty.
Herod	Shall we have some entertainment? Where are the maidens who will dance for the King?

Obed   I shall get them, sir. They are ready and waiting. (*He departs.*)

Asa   Your Majesty, he does look somewhat nervous! He has been saying some strange things recently. (*Perez and Azor look suspiciously at each other. They are familiar with the news.*)

Herod   What strange things? Obed always offers solid advice. See, he was the first to think of exporting goods or selling men in order to bring gold for the King.

Asa   That is true, Your Majesty. Yet I have heard him speak of another… Oh, here they come, sir. (*Enter Obed, followed by girls for dance.*)

Obed   Your Majesty, the beautiful maidens are ready to entertain the King. A new dance suitable for a banquet and set to beautiful music.

Herod   Okay, girls, welcome to the ballroom. You go to work for the King. (*Girls dance to music "A Child Is Born" or other appropriate song referencing the birth of Jesus. Exit afterward.*) Oh, what a fair set of maidens. They always thrill me so much and with a new dance every day. Tell me, Asa, who was it that wrote that piece of music?

Asa   I know not, Your Majesty. I did not enjoy that piece. It is…

Herod   (*angrily*) It was not for you to enjoy. You are but an observer. The music was played for the King. The girls danced for the King.

Azor   Your Majesty, if you will allow me to speak, it will make me happy.

Herod   Words of wisdom or foolish words?

Azor   You will decide, sir…but…but…

Herod
(*angrily*) What is it? Stop the butting lest you butt the Palace down.

Azor
While I listened to and watched, sir, I thought I had a dream, sir. I remember…

Herod
A dream… While you were awake? And standing up? Ha! Ha! (*Laughs vigorously*) Are you numbered among the oxen or the horses? Do you stand while you sleep and dream while you are awake? (*To Obed*) Obed, you bring me more wine. A good laugh deserves another serving.

Obed
At your word, sir. (*Departs*)

Azor
You may continue to laugh, sir, but let me speak. I think I did remember my mother singing a similar tune to mark the birth of a royal babe. No one has been born of your Lady, sir…yet the rumors which we have heard and investigated… I have an uneasy feeling, sir.

Asa
Obed knows all about it, Your Majesty. He has more to tell.

Herod
Is this the same story told by those fools whom have long since died. Let your mind be at ease, Azor… Oh, here comes my wine. (*Obed enters and pours some wine for the king. He sips.*) Ahh… Obed, you know of the rumor…?

Obed
Rumor? I don't believe in rumors, Your Majesty!

Herod
But you have heard that a King's been born. A follow up from an old fable spoken by some foolish fanatics and soothsayers who called themselves Prophets?

Obed
I have heard, sir. I have heard the fable from I was a child. It did not make much sense and still does not.

Azor   That is true, but if this goes out of here, it will stir the people up and there is no way of knowing what will happen.

Herod   This word will never get out of here. This is nonsensical, and I want you all to dismiss it. Forget it now. We shall have no more of this. I want you to swear to it now. All of you.

Asa   I swear it on my word.

Obed   With my whole body, do I swear.

Azor   I so swear. *(Perez remains silent and looks at the king, the king looks back at him.)*

Herod   Have you no word to say, Perez?

Perez   I need not swear, sir, I have not spoken on the matter.

Herod   *(angrily)* Are you defying the orders of the King? Speak! Let me hear you.

Perez   You would not like my words, Your Majesty. I would hate to displease the King.

Herod   If I have to use force, I will get you to speak.

Perez   A king is born, sir, in a stable.

Herod   A King cannot be born in a stable, that's for asses.

Asa   It must be the King of asses, sir. (he laughs)

Azor   You mean the donkey King. *(Laughter increases among all, except for Perez)*

Herod   The donkey King of the horses. You must be right. Ha... Ha... Ha... This is surely comic relief... But did you all swear not to discuss it any further. Bring me some more wine.

Obed   Be careful, Your Majesty, of drunkenness. Your Lady is due at any time now.

Herod   Very well then, I shall have no more wine and we shall not talk anymore about the animal King.

Perez   I did not swear, Your Majesty. I have…

Herod   *(angrily)* Well, swear now.

Perez   Not until I have said my lot. *(Other attendants look at each other with surprise.)*

Perez   The child King is here, but be of good cheer. He shall not interfere with your rule. I had my own dream, and in my dream, I saw the King.

Herod   So you are also a dreamer.

Perez   No, sir, this is while I slept…for three nights.

Herod   *(shouting)* Stop it!

Perez   I swear, sir, my dream has meaning, I know it.

Herod   *(raising his voice even more)* Be gone, you fool, and dream elsewhere. You shall not return to the hall room of the palace until I send for you!

Perez   At your word, sir! *(begins exit, then stops and sings before leaving stage: "A King Is Born")*

A king is born, it has been said

In distant lands as we have read

You may believe or you may not

But all the facts are in the pot

He's come to reign and ease our pain

So, to deny is just in vain

Oh, what a birth! He'll reign on earth

And Herod's rule will have no worth.

There is a God that's up above
Now He's on earth to show His love
His kingdom shall forever last
He shares the future and the past
No sword nor scepter will He need
And yet all peoples He will lead
Oh, what a birth! He'll reign on earth
And Herod's rule will have no worth

Rejoice, rejoice, give thanks and sing
All glory to the new born king
Oh, gentle Jesus, meek and mild
You are a special little child.
We worship and adore you now
To you all earthly kings will bow
Oh what a birth! He'll reign on earth
And Herod's rule will have no worth

Herod	Away with your song. *(shouting)* And stay with your King. *(Perez exits)*
Herod	Is my Lady not coming to the ballroom so I can have some comfort?
Azor	Comfort, Your Majesty? You need no comfort, sir. It's all nonsense.
Herod	Nonsense it is indeed, yet I feel threatened. Will the people still see me as King?

Asa	Unless there is really another King, your throne will last forever. There is only one Royal Family in the land. There is no other King.
Azor	And so, say all of us. Long live the King. Herod is our King. *(All Three)* Long live the King; Herod is our King. *(Enter Tamar, the queen)*
Tamar	Your Majesty, the Queen greets you. What honor is this that you receive?
Herod	Welcome, my Lady; You look really beautiful. Have you heard of rumors?
Tamar	If you are talking about the loss of gold, it is no rumor; it is true and it is all your fault.
Herod	Be calm, my lady. There is no gold, but it is not of gold that I now speak.
Tamar	Well, what rumors are there to be told?
Herod	About a King…a King of… It is so ridiculous.
Tamar	What King? Goodness!
Herod	It has been said that a child has been born and He is to be made King.
Tamar	Are you drunk with wine? You speak foolishly…*(to others)* You may take a stroll young ones… I want to be with his Majesty alone.
All Three	At your word, my Lady. *(All three exit)*
Tamar	You speak the craziest of things when you are drunk. What's flown into your head?
Herod	It is a fact. I am not drunk. I have had no wine for the day.
Tamar	*(pointing at the container)* And what is that at your side?
Herod	*(lifting jug)* Well, I've had a little wine today.

Tamar	So what makes you speak so foolishly?
Herod	I repeat, I do not speak foolishly. Rumor has it that the words of the Prophets of old have come to pass. They spoke of a Messiah. Now we hear of a King. Could they be the same?
Tamar	Do I have to rule in your own Kingdom? Are you going to listen to fables and tales all day long? Your kingdom shall last. These tales have been in circulation from the beginning of time.
Herod	And the fulfillment of the Promise of a Messiah is to come…
Tamar	Listen, Herod. We heard these tales when we were children. When your great-great- grandfather was on the throne he had to deal with them too. Your grandfather had to deal with them too. They read of magicians, soothsayers, and fanatics like Isaiah, Amos, Hosea, idle people who had nothing to do but walk around and stir up confusion. What happened after all this? Nothing…but they discovered that these were a bunch of idiots. Your father too was threatened, but we found out that these were but empty threats. Are these not similar threats? Yes, they are. Very foolish and not even worthy of discussion. Let your mind be at rest and consider how we are going to increase our supply of gold. Are we going to sell men as slaves or are we not?
Herod	You speak as unto a great woman. You are wise. Give me your hand. *(takes her hand)* I will always be King; you will always be my queen.
Tamar	You have spoken well. Will you have some wine?
Herod	One more drink will do me well. *(Sounds horn or gong or other instrument. Perez enters)* I will get the boys. Away with you, you bastard. You are the

one who speaks of another King. Did I not forbid you to come into my presence until I sent for you?

Perez   I heard your horn, Your Majesty. You're still my King.

Herod   Well, it was not for you, you son of a…

Tamar   Do not swear, Your Majesty. Tell me what is his story. *(Azor, Asa, and Obed enters and bows)*

Herod   I forbid him to speak. *(to Perez)* Stand where you are and freeze.
(To Obed) Obed, tell the story of the strange king to my Lady; let her laugh for it is funny.

Tamar   Where is He born?

Asa   In a rotten, smelly stable of a donkey.

Herod   The King of horses we are told, but we'll call Him the donkey King.

Tamar   The story of a manger, I have already heard. But in what country has the so-called mystery happened?

Azor   In Bethlehem of Judah, my Lady.

Obed   I can tell you as it happened or rather as they say it happened.

Herod   You will tell us the story, Obed.

Tamar   And if there is need for firm action, then shall action be taken.

Obed   By your word, my Royal ones, the story I will now unfold. *(all listening intently as he goes downstage, kind of addressing audience.)* In the town of Nazareth of Galilee, there is a beautiful virgin whose name is Mary… She was engaged to Joseph, a carpenter of that same town and then, Your Majesty, according to the story, the strangest thing happened. Before they were married, this virgin became pregnant without a man touching her.

Herod

Oh, utter nonsense. How could such foolish stories be going around?

Asa

There is no need for shock, Your Majesty. There are more foolish things yet.

Obed

The pregnancy, sir, was the work of something called the Holy Ghost or some kind of Spirit.

Tamar

She became pregnant by a Ghost? Can spirits cause conception?

Obed

I don't know, my Lady, but the story continues. Joseph became so suspicious and jealous that he thought of breaking off the engagement. But then he had a dream.

Herod

Another dreamer? I wish someone would dream of gold.

Obed

And in his dream, an angel appeared to him and told him to take home Mary as his wife because it was of the Holy Ghost that she conceived.

Azor

And that's not all, sir. The angel told Joseph that Mary would give birth to a son and that His name would be Jesus, since He would save the people from their sins.

Herod

Do you smell trouble, my Lady?

Tamar

I see trouble brewing, Your Majesty. *(To Azor)* And what did they do? The carpenter and the virgin?

Azor

They got married and had their son.

Tamar

So, if they were from Nazareth, why was the baby born in Bethlehem ? And why should He be seen as King?

Azor

I do not know, my Lady. I've only heard that He is King of the Jews.

Obed

Well, this happened because of the Census which was being taken in the entire Roman world. Everyone had to register, and so Joseph and Mary, even though she was pregnant, had to journey to Bethlehem. It was while she was there that the baby was born. They had gone to the inn, and there was no space there, so they had to resort to the next best thing.

Tamar

And that was a manger?

Obed

Yes, my Lady.

Tamar

(pitifully) Oh, what a dreadful place for a woman to have a baby.

Herod

You're offering sympathy for something that is not true?

Tamar

Well. Just the thought of it is a little sickening.

Asa

But, Your Majesty, the news would have remained there had it not been for some confounded shepherds who claimed that the angel of the Lord led them to the place where the child was. It was they who started to spread the propaganda.

Tamar

I find this extremely frightening. Perhaps we'll have to kill all the shepherds in the land.

Herod

I shall not lift my hand to slay anyone. In a short while, the story will die out, for it will be found to be empty.

Azor

And yet, sir, in my heart, there is this fear…

Herod

There will be no fear. All fears are vanished. Come go and see to the preparation of the banquet hall. Little ones, be calm and let your Majesty handle this affair. *(all depart except Perez , Tamar, and Herod)*

Perez

You see, Your Majesty…

Herod

Oh, Perez, torment me no more. *(To Tamar)* Are you comfortable, my Lady?

Tamar

I shall speak only after this infidel disappears. Can you not rule in your own Kingdom?

Perez

I shall depart, but on my own word. *(Departs)*

Tamar

I am greatly disturbed.

Herod

I am more so.

Tamar

Can you imagine the embarrassment of being forced off one's own throne?

Herod

Who will dare overthrow the King? I shall reign forever.

Tamar

But can it be true?

Herod

I shall appoint ambassadors to Bethlehem now. Let me summon the little ones. *(sounds horns/gong)* I will send men to see if this story is true.

Tamar

And if it is?

Herod

We'll go one step at a time. Three men shall go on our behalf. The wisest men in the land. The most astute and those who are fearless. We must find out before long. *(Attendants enter)*

Asa

What seeks Your Majesty now?

Obed

Ready for service, sir.

Azor

At your word we go!

Herod

Find me three men. Three great men, wise men, brave men. They will go to find the so-called King.

And if they find this King, make sure to bring me
word so I may go to see him too.

Tamar   May the gods help us. Is there another King?

Herod   This is just what we'll find out. There cannot be as
we will see. A child as King? How could this be?

Asa   What news is this?

Azor   What child is this?

Obed   What King is this?

Perez   Where could this be?

(Song "What News Is This" (Herod singing)

What news is this that goes around
That's claiming a new king in town
A baby boy; I'll shut Him down
Now don't you think I am a clown
I'll search and search till he be found
I'll strike Him dead and those around
This must be stopped; I'll say it now
It's just to me that you must bow.

What child is this who lives that way
Among the cattle, sheep, and hay
He dares not show his face today
He needs a hiding place to stay
So strike, strike with your swords and spears
Please be at peace and calm your fears
I'm still not sure if this is true
But just in case, we'll follow through

What king is this who wears no crown

And neither has thrones nor palace?
He lives among the cows and lambs
And swine and donkeys and horses
Not one child can replace a king
It is my throne and here's my ring
My rule will never have an end
But yet some wise men, I will send.

Where could this be, I want to know
For I may be the first to go
He must be slain I want Him dead
No crown shall be upon His head
So let's rejoice and drink more wine
For everything will be just fine
Cheers and more Cheers rejoice with me
I am the king and will always be.

(Exit And Curtain)

ACT I, SCENE 3
The Home of Luke and Martha

By now, he is a grown man and has his family. With him are his wife, mother, and sister. His mother's name is Susanna, wife is Martha, and sister is Virginia. Susanna and Martha are doing housework.

Narrator/Voice *(off-stage)*	And before long, the news had spread all over the land and the mysterious birth of the newborn King was the talk of the town. In every home, there were people trying to understand the mystery. Some believed and some did not. People listened keenly to hear the voice of the heralds so as to hear the updates.
Martha	Mom, it is such an unbelievable thing and yet it is true. But can it be true?
Susanna	It was foretold, my dear, by the Prophets of old, but I tell you this *(Whispers)* The people of this town are unbelieving and Virginia is one of them.

Martha   Virginia doesn't believe it, eh? I wonder when she is going to cease being so doubtful.

Susanna   In her mind, all the people of the town have gone crazy. The heralds all seem to have taken a dose of hot pepper soup. They have all gone mad, mad, mad.

Martha   Well, let me be a fool or even be called mad, but I believe in the Holy Scriptures. The word of God has come to pass. You remember, Mom, that the scriptures did speak of a Messiah. One from the rod of Jesse and the line of David who would save his people from their sins.

Susanna   Yes, this relates to what the Prophet Jeremiah wrote, "The time is coming saith the Lord when I will make a new covenant with the house of Israel and with the house of Judah…for I will forgive their wickedness and remember their sins no more." My dear, now that the savior is born, the Lord will not deal with us according to our iniquities.

Martha   Oh! To God be the glory, great things He hath done. He so loves this world that He has given us His son. I can't believe it; the Messiah is here at last.

Susanna   So you do think it is the expected Messiah, the anointed one of God?

Martha   Of course, who else could it be? Everything seems to be falling in place just as the scripture has it. His name shall be called Emmanuel for God is with us. Emmanuel! Emmanuel! Emmanuel! Emmanuel! *(Sings "Oh, Come, Oh Come Emmanuel.") (After this, Virginia is to enter, she can be seen by Susanna before she comes on stage)*

Susanna   Oh, here comes the great unbeliever, Virginia is coming.

Martha	Is she really? *(Virginia enters)* Virginia, have you heard any more news about this newborn King?
Virginia	If you are talking about the idle rumors, I have nothing to report, save what I heard from the heralds a few minutes ago.
Susanna	They are not idle rumors, my daughter. You must believe the word of God.
Virginia	As far as I am concerned, this whole town has gone crazy and we seem to be short of psychiatrists. I listened to the message of the heralds moments ago and…let me tell you both something. Herod is going to be declaring war on everyone who believes this nonsense. The country's going to be divided.
Martha	Oh! For crying out loud, what is all this? That sounds like madness.
Susanna	Well, Herod is crazy enough to do anything. Do you remember the massacre which was…?
Virginia	Well, it may be crazy, but it is madness versus madness. Perhaps we should keep the monitor on so that we can get up to the minute reports. The reports will continue to come through the voice of the heralds.
Martha	Right. *(monitor goes off)* Wait, listen! Listen!
Susanna	It has never been like this in this country.
Virginia	Shhhhh!
Herald's Voice	*(offstage)* But after several interviews were made with different people, there is still no consensus as to whether or not these statements should be treated merely as rumors. Meanwhile, reports coming in from the Palace of King Herod say that there is fire and fury and indignation raging in every corner of the Palace. King Herod is said to have sent

astrologers who have studied the stars to find out exactly where the baby is born. These wise men were guided by a star and it is alleged that they, in fact, found the babe lying in a manger in swaddling clothes…

Martha

So it is true. I told you.

Virginia

Shut up, you fool, and listen! Don't you know that Herod will take your neck?

Herald's Voice

However, Herod's indignation was heightened when he heard that the wise men have f led to another country after finding the babe and presenting Him with gifts of gold and frankincense and myrrh. His anger has resulted in sleepless nights, and at the Palace there is a mixture of confusion and fury.

Virginia

Oh, I will not take any more of this. We will have to make an effort not to be a part of all this nonsense. *(Luke enters. He is full of glee.)*

Luke

All ye ladies rejoice and be glad. The redeemer has come! Let us be merry and set sorrow aside; Christ Jesus our Savior was born on this tide.

Virginia

Another fanatic! Oh Lord, is there one more person in this town with basic common sense? Why me alone, Lord? Luke, are you believing this too?

Luke

Yes, of course it is true. I told you that you were to expect all of this. I heard about it from the mouth of the Prophet when I was younger, but I could not understand it very well then. Yet I vaguely remember him telling me about the promised Messiah. Ever since that, I have been dreaming, hoping, longing, and expecting this Messiah. And now, my dream is coming true. The dream of all the Prophets has come true.

Virginia   But you're still dreaming, we have not seen Him yet.

Susanna   Not seen whom? The King?

Martha   He is born and He is Savior too. The King of all Kings.

Luke   Listen, ladies, let me tell you all about it. Just how it started in my life and why it continues to be a part of my life. It all started when I was young. Very, very young, and I met the Prophet then I started my dream.

(Sings "A Dream Come True.")

I had a dream when I was young
The prophet spoke to me
He said the virgin shall conceive
And give birth to a son
God's own son will come on earth
And the Messiah we shall see
In Him, we'll place our hopes and dreams
And now my dream has just come true.

There is a sign which you will see
Is what he said to me
He shall be called Immanuel
He'll rule the earth so well
Curds and honey, He will eat
That little one will be so sweet
How great to know He'll love me so
And now my dream has just come true.

For now, to us a child is born,

To us God's son is here

Name Him Everlasting Father

Wonderful Counsellor

Mighty God and Prince of Peace

He'll surely reign on David's throne

Upholding it forevermore

And now my dream has just come true.

Virginia	*(sarcastically)* Some dream come true. Do you all think that this is going to be circulated for long? Never! By the time…
Luke	This truth will never fade, but will last forever, because the King will live forever! Every minute, we hear of some more news that has been added. The latest is about the shepherds! Did you hear about them how they saw the angels?
Susanna	No, my son; tell us about that.
Martha	What shepherds? You mean those who owned the Manger where He was born?
Luke	No. I tell you this is so fantastic because it is sheer coincidence. I heard that the same night in which this King was born, and the shepherds were busy with their work, a bright light shone…
Virginia	*(sarcastically)* And they hallucinated!
Luke	Will you give me a chance to finish, you unbeliever? It was the angel of the Lord who had appeared and the whole glory of the Lord shone round about them. Can you imagine how fearful they were? They nearly died.
Martha	So did they run?

Luke	Yes, run they did, but it was following the news. They ran straight to where the young child was.
Susanna	And did they see Him? I bet they did.
Luke	Of course, they helped to spread the news when they saw Him.
Martha	Oh, I wish that I was there.
Susanna	Me too! Luke, can you take us there?
Virginia	You may end up in Herod's prison cells. If you continue to believe this. Let me get out of this place so that when Herod's Armies come, I will not be taken.
Luke	When Christ's Armies come, you may not be taken either.
Virginia	*(leaving)* Convince yourselves. Don't try to convince me. *(she leaves)*
Susanna	My poor daughter. She has always asked for signs of proof before she believes anything.
Luke	Let her alone, Mom. She will accept in due course. All of us will someday.
Martha	But, Luke, how can we really say that the king was born in a manger? Is that a place for Kings?
Luke	You see, He is different from other Kings. This is what the Prophets told us. He is meek and lowly, humble, and obedient. He was born in a lowly manger, yet His reign shall be over all the earth.
Susanna	And that was why He was conceived of the Holy Ghost and not by normal means. He just has to be different. This proves your medical knowledge wrong, son!
Luke	No, Mom. I am a doctor all right, but now I do not speak as a doctor. I speak as a believer. I know that

it does sound strange for a babe to be born in the way we've been told He was, but God had to make Him special. And special He is going to be.

Martha   I believe it. Every word is true. Are you going to take us there? Even if it takes us many days?

Susanna   We will load the camels with food and water and we shall start out on our way to Bethlehem.

Luke   Let us all go. Why not? Everyone else is going! Let us go and praise Him too.

Martha   Oh great! Hail thou ever blessed morn.

Susanna   Hail redemption's happy dawn.

Martha and Susanna   Sing through all Jerusalem.

Luke   Christ is born in Bethlehem.

(they sing "See Amid the Winter's Snow")

See amid the winter's snow
Born for us on earth below
See the tender Lamb appears
Promised from eternal years

CHO
Hail, thou ever blessed morn
Hail, redemption's happy dawn
Sing through all Jerusalem
Christ is born in Bethlehem
Say, ye holy shepherds, say
What your joyful news today
Wherefore have ye left your sheep
On the lonely mountain steep?

CHO
Hail, thou ever blessed morn
Hail, redemption's happy dawn
Sing through all Jerusalem
Christ is born in Bethlehem
Sacred infant, all divine
What a tender love was thine
Thus, to come from highest bliss
Down to such a world as this

CHO
Hail, thou ever blessed morn
Hail, redemption's happy dawn
Sing through all Jerusalem
Christ is born in Bethlehem
Hail, thou ever blessed morn
Hail, redemption's happy dawn
Sing through all Jerusalem
Christ is born in Bethlehem
(End of scene)

ACT II, SCENE 1
The Home of Joseph and Mary

Joseph's two younger brothers also live with them. One is Mark and the other is Aaron. Mary is sewing while Joseph is mixing milk for the baby.

Joseph	*(taking pot over to Mary)* This should be ready now, Mary. Thick and rich. Our boy shall grow fast.
Mary	Looks all right. Do you think that you could feed Him?
Joseph	But he is still asleep. Let Him get some rest for when he grows, it will be hard work all his days.
Mary	That is so true. Joseph, why would God choose a lowly maiden like me to bring the Savior into this world?
Joseph	Well, I am a poor carpenter. Why should I be called his father? But God will raise up the poor and humble; while those who are mighty may fall.
Mary	That God should choose to use me, I'll never understand. *(repeats words of the Magnificat, verse speaking)*

My soul magnifies the Lord

And my spirit rejoices in God my Savior;

Because He has regarded the lowliness of His handmaid; For behold, henceforth all generations shall call me blessed; Because He who is mighty has done great things for me,

and holy is His name;

And His mercy is from generation to generation

The Home of Mary and Joseph on those who fear Him. He has shown might with His arm,

He has scattered the proud in the conceit of their heart.

He has put down the mighty from their thrones, and has exalted the lowly. He has filled the hungry with good things, and the rich He has sent away empty.

He has given help to Israel, his servant, mindful of His mercy

Even as he spoke to our fathers, to Abraham and to his posterity forever.

(Mark and Aaron enters with a buzz of excitement)

Aaron	Joseph, Mary! Guess what! Poor news from…
Joseph	Shhhh! The baby is asleep.
Mark	But they are going to kill Him.
Mary	Don't say that! You make me tremble!
Mark	Well, it is true. King Herod is killing all the infant boys.
Joseph	The child King must be awake now… What did you say, Mark? Herod is killing…

Aaron	All the newborn male children. Since he cannot identify exactly which child is the threat to his throne, he's going to take them all, saying that the King must be slaughtered among the number.
Joseph	Herod is wicked enough to do this.
Mary	*(bursting into tears)* Oh Lord! I can't take this. Let it not be so.
Mark	Don't cry, big sister. Don't cry please. *(Starts to cry too)*
Mary	Out of the depths I cry to thee, Oh Lord. Lord, hear my voice. Let thine ears be attentive to the voice of my supplications.
Aaron	Do you think that God would let Herod destroy the child King? Do you remember what David wrote about God many years ago…a refuge and shield?
Mark	Yes, I remember. God is my refuge and strength. A very present help in trouble.
Aaron	Therefore, we will not fear, though the earth be removed and though the mountains be carried into the midst of the sea.
Joseph	Though the waters thereof roar and be troubled, though the mountains shake with the swelling thereof; there is a river, the streams whereof shall make glad the City of God, the Holy Place of the tabernacle of the Most High. *(Joseph completes remainder of Psalms 46 from Verse 5 to end as solo verse speaking)*

God is within her, she will not fall;

God will help her at break of day.

Nations are in uproar, kingdoms fall;

he lifts his voice, the earth melts

The Lord Almighty is with us;

the God of Jacob is our fortress.

Come and see what the Lord has done,

the desolations he has brought on the earth.

He makes wars cease

to the ends of the earth.

He breaks the bow and shatters the spear;

he burns the shields[d] with fire.

He says, "Be still, and know that I am God;

I will be exalted among the nations,

I will be exalted in the earth."

The Lord Almighty is with us;

the God of Jacob is our fortress.

Mark	Well, aren't we going to hide the little baby?
Mary	Not after the reassurance given by David's song. The Lord will protect the child. He belongs to Him, and we have only been asked to care for him.
Aaron	Well, if God wants us to care for Him, we need to protect him from Herod's men. I heard that several babies were innocently killed in the town next to ours. Within a week, we could lose our precious little king.
Joseph	I think I hear the Lord speaking to me. Do you know what I dreamt last night?
Mark	*(Sarcastically)* Joseph, the dreamer, dreams again.
Joseph	It is no joke. I dreamt that which I could not understand…now I can understand.

Aaron	Well, tell us. Please! Did you dream that someone died?
Mary	He could not have dreamt that!
Joseph	If you will only listen. I dreamt that I was alone with the Lord our God. He took me on a far journey that looked so long. While we were walking, I did not know where we were going or why we were going. I only followed.
Mark	On and on.
Joseph	Yes, on and on until we came to the end of the journey and we sat down to rest. Then he talked.
Aaron	What did he say?
Mary	Aaron, be patient! He is going to tell us.
Joseph	He told me that he had taken me there for a purpose. I was to protect all his people. "You are in charge," the Lord said, "and remember the little one."
Aaron and Mark	The little one?
Joseph	He asked me not to leave the place until he told me to; for only if I remained would I be able to protect his people.
Mark	And what does this dream mean?
Joseph	I don't know, perhaps the Lord wants us to leave this place.
Aaron	How could we leave Jesus alone? Who would protect him?
Joseph	No, we would not leave him alone, we would take him with us.
Mary	Oh, Joseph, I couldn't take anymore. After that long journey to Bethlehem and the long journey

back. I think I have done enough traveling for two years.

Joseph

(frustratingly) Well, it's for your own good and the baby's. Haven't you heard that Herod is going to kill him? Do you want to stay here and sacrifice your blood?

Mary

You don't have to shout, Joseph. *(the baby cries from inside)* And that's it! The baby is up.

Joseph

I lost my temper, didn't I? Yes! How unnecessary. I am sorry, Mary. This dream is affecting me so much!

Mary

But you are human too. You will lose your temper even if you are to be known as father of the Lord's anointed. I'll go inside to see if the baby is all right. *(she moves inside singing a lullaby)*

Mark

You mean that we will have to pack up everything and go away?

Aaron

All because of Herod that wicked king! If I ever catch Herod, I would tie his hands and feet and beat him all over.

Joseph

Be careful, Aaron. If Herod's men were to hear you say that, they would cut you down the middle; they would cut you right in two.

Mark

Where are we going, big brother, if we leave here?

Aaron

Are we going far?

Joseph

Not if we leave here. We will have to leave and the best place to go is into Egypt.

Mark and Aaron

Egypt?

Joseph

Yes, Egypt! According to my understanding of the dream, this is where the Lord wants us to go. *(Mary enters)*

Mary	The baby is all right. It just seems to have been a little too cold for him.
Mark	We are going to Egypt. Joseph just told us.
Mary	Of all the places to go! The land of the slaves.
Joseph	Just being obedient to the angel of the Lord. That's all.
Aaron	When shall we leave?
Mary	No, no, Aaron, let Joseph and I take the baby, it would be too risky for all of us to leave this house and go all the way to Egypt.
Aaron	I want to go!
Mark	Me too, I may never see you again.
Joseph	You will see us. The Lord will protect us and He will protect you. Boys, I think Mary is right. You stay and keep watch.
Mary	We could get your Aunt Ruth to come stay with you. She will help to keep you company and do all the chores.
Mark	Auntie Ruth! Oh, that's marvelous.
Aaron	We'll stay then. *(Confidently)* We can fight. *(Speaks boisterously).* If Herod and his men come I will just…bip, bip, bip, boop, boop, baf! *(demonstrates with his fists a fighting spirit)*
Mark	And I will kick him with my feet! *(all chuckle)*
Joseph	Mary, we will have to make great haste. We cannot delay for too long.
Mary	I know that. Let me begin to get the things together. The Lord is surely a deliverer. He has sent Jesus to deliver all people from their sins. Now He is

delivering the same Jesus from the hands of wicked men.

Joseph   They will never find us in Egypt, and that's where we are bound. Look out, Egypt, we are coming.

(Sings with Mary "To Egypt We Go")

To Egypt, to Egypt, to Egypt we go;
My wife and little baby boy; to Egypt we go
King Herod won't find us, to Egypt we go
We place ourselves in our God's hands, to Egypt we go.

Herod has been searching, to Egypt we go
But we will just protect God's child, to Egypt we go
We will not wait; we've got to go; to Egypt we go
And we won't stop till we get there; to Egypt we go

We have no food but we don't care; to Egypt we go
Jehovah Jireh; God still cares; to Egypt we go
The road seems dark but still we trod; to Egypt we go
Our child will be the light from God; to Egypt we go.

So let us not worry; to Egypt we go
Instead, we'll be merry; to Egypt we go
We're packed and we're ready; to Egypt we go
Take care and God Bless you; to Egypt we go.

To Egypt, to Egypt to Egypt we go;
My wife and little baby boy; to Egypt we go
King Herod won't find us, to Egypt we go
We place ourselves in our God's hands, to Egypt we go.

Voice/Narrator   And after thorough preparation that looked so long, they were ready to start on their journey. They took up the baby Jesus, and off they went with Mark and Aaron left alone.

Aaron	Aren't you sad that Auntie Ruth isn't coming?
Mark	I am sad. Us two alone. How boring this will be.
Aaron	Oh boy! Can't you find something more to say? No baby to look at. We can't keep the door open; we can't look through the window.
Mark	Did Mary and Joseph really mean that?
Aaron	Mean what?
Mark	That we should keep all the windows and doors locked tight. How could they!
Aaron	Of course, they meant it. If Herod's men know that people live in here, they will burn the house down unless we open the doors.
Mark	And if we are locked in here, we will be burnt too. May God help us.
Aaron	He will! Oh, God, thou art, my God; early will I seek thee.

(Repeats Psalm 63:1–8)

You, God, are my God,

earnestly I seek you;

I thirst for you,

my whole being longs for you,

in a dry and parched land

where there is no water.

I have seen you in the sanctuary

and beheld your power and your glory.

Because your love is better than life,

my lips will glorify you.

I will praise you as long as I live,

and in your name I will lift up my hands.

I will be fully satisfied as with the richest of foods;

with singing lips my mouth will praise you.

On my bed I remember you;

I think of you through the watches of the night.

Because you are my help,

I sing in the shadow of your wings.

I cling to you;

your right hand upholds me.

Voice/Narrator	And after some time, a noise was heard from outside.
Aaron	Did you hear the noise? *(Noise from outside)*
Mark	No, you are dreaming.
Aaron	Come listen.
Mark	Oh, that must be… (Luke's voice from outside)
Luke	Ho! What ho?
Mark	Lord, save us! (As they try to hide)
Aaron	Go and answer or they'll burn us in fire.
Mark	You shut up, why don't you answer?
Luke	What ho! What ho! Is there anybody home? *(the two boys look at each other trembling hard)* Is there anyone home? We need to see the king!

Mark	There is no king here, and besides, nobody lives here.
Luke	Well, can I come in?
Aaron	Did you hear, there is no one here. No one lives here.
Mark	Go away. Persons live next door.
Luke	We want to see Jesus!
Aaron	He is gone to Egypt.
Mark	Shhhhhhh! Idiot!
Aaron	Jesus lives in the house down the road. (they look at each other again, persons now come nearer)
Luke	Is this the house of Mary and Joseph? (boys can now see person)
Aaron	I see who it is. It is a man and a woman.
Mark	But the woman wouldn't kill Jesus? What is your name, sir?
Luke	My name is Luke. We have come from far. We want to see Jesus.
Mark	*(to Aaron)* Let's open the door. *(Aaron opens door)* Your name is Luke?
Luke	Yes, and this is my mother Susanna and my wife Martha.
Aaron	If you have come to see Jesus, you have come to the wrong place.
Martha	But we've heard that this is where the infant king is.
Mark	Do you want to kill him?
Luke	Of course not. We only want to get to know him and worship him.

Susanna	You see we believe that He is the Messiah, and we were waiting for Him to come. And now we would like to look at His face. Is he here? *(the boys look at each other again)*
Aaron	It seems that you have had a long journey. Would you like to have something to drink?
Luke	No, we just want to see the child king. Are Mary and Joseph here?
Mark	Do you know Herod?
Martha	Of course, we do. Well…we have heard of him.
Susanna	What is it about Herod?
Mark	Did he send you here?
Luke	Well…why? We have never even been near the palace.
Mark	Well, Herod is after Jesus. He is trying to destroy all the male children born in Bethlehem. Within the last four days…
Luke	So he killed Jesus?
Aaron	No, but Jesus…
Mark	Mary and Joseph took Jesus down to Egypt.
Susanna	Down to Egypt?
Mark	Yes, to save him from Herod's men.
Martha	But we have to see Him. That's why we've come.
Aaron	Well, you can only see Him if you go to Egypt.
Susanna	Oh no! (Susanna and Martha look at each other) Martha!
Mark	Or you can wait here until they get back.
Luke	So they are coming back? Do you know when?

Mark	I suppose, when he is big enough to run from Herod.
Martha	That might be too long. What a misery?
Susanna	And you're here by yourselves?
Aaron	No! God is with us. Did you know that Jesus is also called Emmanuel? This means that "God is with us."
Susanna	Emanuel! Emanuel! We're going to find you one day.
Mark	You're going to Egypt?
Luke	That's the only way we can find him. But we will find Him. Ladies, shall we continue our journey?
Martha	All this waste, it could just…
Luke	No, it's not a waste. God will help us find him.
Mark	Are you leaving now?
Susanna	We must be going, for we must find this Jesus.
Aaron	Bye now.
Martha and Susanna	Take care of yourselves now
Luke	We'll see you. (They depart. Boys look at each other.)
Mark	Man! I thought my life was finished!
Aaron	You mean that I am still alive!
Mark	Well, they weren't going to hurt us.
Aaron	I know, but they scared me badly.
Mark	God is so merciful. My mouth shall continually sing forth His praise. (Begins to sing (unacompanied) "O Little Town of Bethlehem" first two verses)

Voice/Narrator   After the trauma of that experience was over, it was soon to be relived. After some time, Herod's men finally got to the house. *(By this time, they are both offstage.)*

First Speaker   *(from outside)* Will all housekeepers open their doors? The king has a message to deliver.

Aaron   *(running on stage)* Who is it? What do you want?

First Speaker   *(nearer)* We are from the palace of Herod. We have a present for all the newborn babies. May we come in?

Aaron   Well, there are no babies here. You could try next door.

Second Speaker   Have you heard of one Joseph and his wife Mary? Aaron No, I've not heard of them! Have you?

Second Speaker   We want to find them and their son. Are you going to let us in? *(Goes to open the door to let men in. Mark comes out looking Curiously, men also enter)* Where is the baby?

Mark   Why does everyone want to see a baby? Can't you see that we are alone here?

Aaron   But you may leave a present with us.

First Speaker   You would not like it. Our presents are only for babies.

Mark   How mean you are. Okay, keep your present. I hope you won't find any babies to give them to.

First Speaker   We'll see about that. Hey, there's no time to waste, we must be about the king's business.

Mark   You'll have to leave?

Second Speaker   Yes, it is a long and tedious job that we have to do. We must be gone.

Aaron   Go with God.

Second Speaker   What did you say?

Mark   He said God will go with you. Depart in peace.
                         First Speaker   In peace we go. *(Both exit)*

Voice/Narrator: And for the second time, Aaron and Mark
                         overcame their fear and so they sang "All Glory

Laud and Honor." (they sing first two verses and chorus)

CHO

All glory, laud, and honor
to you, Redeemer, King,
to whom the lips of children
made sweet hosannas ring.
You are the King of Israel
and David's royal Son,
now in the Lord's name coming,
the King and Blessed One.

The company of angels
is praising you on high;
and we with all creation
in chorus make reply.

CHO
All glory, laud, and honor
to you, Redeemer, King,
to whom the lips of children
made sweet hosannas ring.

(End of scene)

ACT II, SCENE 2
The Palace of Herod

There is embitterment and frustration as Herod's plans have failed. Herod and Tamar are sitting together in the security room. Tamar is his queen.

Tamar	The men have fled? But they could never do that?
Herod	All three of them. A wretched set. *(pause)* But they will have to flee for life. They would never be able to bear the punishment that I shall inflict upon them.
Tamar	You may never find them, Herod.
Herod	Unless they were already dead. If they make their beds in hell, I will find them there.
Tamar	I wonder if it could be that they have not yet found the infant king?
Herod	What infant king? Are you out of your mind?
Tamar	I beg your pardon. I mean the so-called infant king.
Herod	They did find him. In that old dirty stable filled with animal waste and smelling like a rotten fruit.
Tamar	Well…so they should have come back to report to you…but they didn't.

Herod

No, they did not. The news I received is that they fell down and worshipped him. They greeted him royally as if he were really king.

Tamar

Well then, perhaps he is! Could it be…?

Herod

Nonsense! Stop it, you're filled with wine. Are you one to overthrow your own husband?

Tamar

Calm down, Your Majesty. Your throne is not threatened. So what if he were thought to be King? He is still an infant so that you would continue to rule for a long time.

Herod

And what would happen to our son? Is there not a place for him on my throne? Of course, there is. Herod the Second shall take over as king when I die. No carpenter or any carpenter's son shall rule in Judea; it is only those from the seed of Herod, and it was in order to make sure of this that I have asked that all the newborn males be slain. The blood will continue to flow until I become convinced that this boy is dead.

Tamar

What confusion this is going to cause in the land?

Herod

There will be no confusion after he is slain along with those who are supposed to be his mother and father.

Tamar

Herod, I wish to see you continue as king for as long as you are able. I would want to see my son on the throne. When you are on the throne… when you are on the throne, I will be queen. When I am queen, there will be more gold for me. When there is gold, I will…

Herod

Gold? Gold? There is no gold…gold? There won't be much for you my queen even if I remain on the throne.

Tamar	But why? Aren't you in control? I know that the gold in the land is depleting, but I would want to see the palace lined with more gold even before the stocks were depleted.
Herod	Tamar my queen. Let me not grieve you. Yet I will have to grieve you, for I am grieved too. Those three scoundrels whom we thought were wise turned out to be foolish. Of all things that they did…they presented gold to the…
Tamar	They did what?
Herod	Gave away gold, which is already in short supply to the child. Three gifts they presented to the child's mother. Gold, Frankincense, and Myrrh.
Tamar	*(shouting)* No, they did not!
Herod	Yes, they did. What more can one ask for? *(two attendants, Azor and Obed, enter)* My word, this is fast. What word do you bring? Is it good news for the palace?
Obed	The news, Your Majesty, is not very pleasant.
Tamar	Oh, please, I cannot take anymore unpleasant news! What is it?
Herod	There is nothing unpleasant, my Lady, that the emperor cannot deal with.
Obed	Your Majesty, we have examined the reports of those who were sent out to kill the newborn babies. So far, approximately, for hundred and fifty thousand bodies have been burnt…
Herod	Oh, great news. There is a reward for all the men. Bring them in. *(Tamar smiles at this)*
Obed	But, Your Majesty, there is not yet any guarantee that this so-called infant king is among them. In fact, it is thought that some babies fled.

Tamar	Some babies fled? I thought it was the astrologers who fled.
Herod	It was the astrologers who fled.
Obed	That is true, Your Majesty but this is in the news that I received and I now pass on to you. As the men went from house to house, they found the house of Mary and Joseph, the parents of this special babe. But only two grown boys were found there. They later discovered that Mary and Joseph had taken the child on a flight to some distant land.
Herod	To what distant land did they flee?
Obed	No one knows, Your Majesty.
Herod	Azor, do you know? But why did they f lee? Did they know that men were after them?
Azor	I know nothing, My Lord.
Tamar	There must be some supreme power at work for them.
Herod	There is no supreme power but mine. I rule this land. Everyone falls under my command.
Tamar	Well, find them! *(PAUSE)* Your Majesty, you may as well give up the fight.
Herod	There is no fight. I am king and I shall continue to be king.
Tamar	And if you are king, why all the fuss? Stay calm and relax for no one can overthrow you.
Herod	Well, I am filled with torment.
Tamar	Because you are not a real king. No real king would feel threatened by a baby taking over his throne. *(Asa enters)*

Asa   Your Majesties, Your Majesties. What are you going to do? Half the country is marching on the streets and a few have gone down to Egypt, it is said that's where the new king is.

Herod   *(angrily)* What is all this? Stop the confusion. Everyone stop it! Do you all hear me?

Asa   You will have to stop it, Your Majesty. You are King but those persons on the streets no longer think so. They have been singing and shouting for "Jesus the Name High Over All" and "Born is the King of Israel." Glory to the newborn king.

Herod   *(angrily)* I will kill all of you.

Tamar   Start with yourself, dear king. I tell you these things are not ordinary. Perhaps we should bow to the greater powers.

Herod   Bow to the greater powers? The greater powers will bow to me!

Asa   Your Majesty, if only you had heard them; you would not have said that. Those who went down to Egypt kept singing on their way "O come let us adore him, Christ the Lord" and "Worship Christ the newborn king." Your Majesty, they have all been sold to the idea that this infant is King. It is Him whom they worship. It is him they've gone to see… It is Him who will be King.

Herod   It is Him who will die.

Tamar   He is not going to die. I am terrified too. With those powers, anything can happen to us. Something may befall us in this Palace.

Asa   And, sir, to make the situation a little more frightening, one of our own has been out on the streets with them joining in the march. Perez, Your Majesty…

Herod   Perez is there too! *(calmly)* Ah! *(Angrily)* That double-tongued bastard! He is a traitor! He too shall die.

Azor   Your Majesty, if it pleases you, I will go to find Perez and bring him back here so that he can show his sorrow. I do not want him to die.

Herod   You want to run away too. Oh! No, Azor, I do not trust anyone here, I do not want you to go.

Tamar   You do not trust anyone. You have lost confidence in yourself. And just as well too. Your powers as King are diminishing rapidly. The whole country will soon turn against you.

Asa   Dear king. If you are losing power as king, you can regain such power. Send all the messengers out; let them tell the people that you now have a lot of gold in the country. Then they will honor and respect you as king.

Obed   Then, sir, you will get them back on your side.

Azor   But you won't keep them for long. For what will they do when they find out that there is no gold?

Tamar   I say, they will become so indignant that they may turn further away. We should bow to the greater powers. I have spoken. *(gets up to leave)*

Obed   Oh no, my Lady, you cannot leave until you help us to solve this problem.

Asa   How do we establish sovereignty in this Palace?

Tamar   We need someone with great power and authority to do this and my husband here is lacking in this.

Herod   So you have turned against me too.

Tamar   I am not against you. You are still my husband, but I cannot be sure you are my king.

Herod	*(angrily)* Then who is your king? Is it the old carpenter's son, born in the stable? Is it that little brat whose parents have the magical powers? Can a child be your king?
Tamar	You will be the wiser to worship the King.
Herod	You have gone out of your mind. Asa, who is your king? Azor, who is your king? Obed, who is your king? Tell her now who is your king, for I know that I am king. *(all remain silent)* Who is your king? *(Still silence) (Softly)* You will not answer me.
Tamar	I know the answer, Herod, or rather I know not the answer. I may not know who is their king, but I know who their king is not.
Herod	Men, speak for yourselves.
Azor	The queen has spoken, sir.
Herod	But you, what do you say for yourself?
Obed	She has spoken for me, sir.
Asa	Me too, sir.
Herod	She has spoken for you, so I am not your king. I do not have any rule. Well, then we shall see. Tamar, you sit down for a while. All three of you pull your swords. *(They pull their swords)* I want **you to kill** each other. *(Asa makes after Obed and stops)*
Asa	No, sir. We have always worked with each other
Herod	Matters not. Work against each other now.
Azor	Your Majesty…
Herod	It is either you die or I shall die. Put the swords in me. If anyone thinks that I am not fit to be king, he does not deserve to live. If everyone feels the same way, then I do not deserve to live.

Tamar   Very soon, you will not deserve to live.

Obed   A king would not want to die.

Azor   You cannot be king, sir.

Asa   What king is this?

Tamar   What king is this?

All   What king is this?
                 (all except Herod sing "What King Is This" part 2
                 message/song   intended   for   audience   at
                 appropriate places in song)

What king is this who's lost his throne
And cannot rule within this town
He will give up his earthly throne
For by a child, he's been overthrown
Tell me tell me what will you do
For shedding blood will not help you
Let's all go and worship now
For to this new king, we all must bow

You have no place, you've lost your pow'r
You have to go at any hour
So pack your bags and let us go
And do not make this child your foe
You will never be drinking wine
Nor at the golden table you'll dine
Thanks to God for this new birth
His own son to rule upon this earth

Do not fret about your sin

For in your heart, He'll enter in

I'm glad you're here to hear this news

No more this world will be confused

For salvation has come to man

For It is a part of our God's plan

Open up your hearts today

And take the savior while you may.

(End scene)

ACT II, SCENE 3
The Home of Joseph and Mary

Mary has the baby in her arms.

Mary

I'll never know how to thank God for honoring me so. I do not deserve to be the mother of such a great king.

Joseph

Mary, please! Do not disturb the Spirit of the Lord. He has guided and protected us so well. You see how He led us down to Egypt and back? Give that boy to me! *(Mary gives the baby to Joseph) (To baby)* Hey, little one. Your name is Jesus. You are the Christ and you are the king. Did you know that? *(Mary smiles)* Yea, you are.

Mary

Oh, he's so cute.

Joseph

And guess what little one! They nearly killed you! We had to rescue you from Herod. We had to take you all the way into Egypt, and now here we are. Alone and free.

Mary

Well, we're not free yet. Are we? I don't think that we are out of Herod's grasp.

Joseph   Perhaps we are not, but the God who has been protecting us will continue to do so.
(Gives the baby back to Mary)

Mary   Oh, come, sweet little one. *(Sings him a lullaby. Toward the end, there is a knock on the door. It is Luke, Martha, and Virginia)* That must be someone else waiting to see you, Baby Jesus. Joseph, are we ever going to stop having visitors? Is this the price I have to pay for being the mother of a king? *(Knock is heard again. Joseph goes to answer.)* We must have had a thousand visitors since Jesus was born. *(all three enter)*

Luke   Greetings, holy mother, and to your little son. I'll say "Hail the Heaven born Prince of Peace, Hail the Son of Righteousness."

Mary   Oh, thank you, kind sir. I don't deserve all this.

Luke   Of course, you do. The birth of this babe has meant that my dream has come true… Words of the father, now in flesh appearing.

Joseph   What means all of this?

Martha   Oh, excuse him please, sir. He is so excited for he heard about the promise when he was young.

Joseph   But who are you? You may at least introduce yourself.

Virginia   Let me start with me. *(pointing to Luke)* I will start with him. His name is Luke. The prophet appeared to him when he was quite young and told him to expect the birth of the Messiah. For him, it is really a dream come true. Luke is my brother and she *(pointing to Martha)* is Martha, his wife. She too is excited about the birth of the King.

Mary   Joseph! Isn't this fantastic?

Joseph   It is marvelous.

Virginia	And I am Virginia, their sister. I did not believe when I heard it at first. I thought that it was nonsense and said that the entire world had gone mad. But now I am convinced. It is true. I have seen him with my own eyes. This day, I have seen the salvation of the Lord. Yippee! *(to audience)* You can find Jesus too. I hope that you have all witnessed the Salvation of the Lord. If not, I urge you to seek him now. *(Mary and Joseph look at each other)*
Martha	Did you know that this is our second trip here? Yes! Luke and I and our mother came all this way to see the child. We were met by two little boys who told us that you were gone to Egypt, but we were so excited, we still had to make the journey to Egypt, but we missed you again.
Luke	Our mother, Susanna, traveled with us, but she is too tired now, she could not make the journey again.
Mary	Well, this is wonderful.
Luke	Just what the prophet told us. His name shall be called Wonderful, Counselor, Mighty God, Prince of Peace.
Joseph	Mary, perhaps you should put the baby down and get our friends some food to eat.
Mary	I'll do just that. (puts the baby into crib and goes for food)
Joseph	You know, sometimes it is difficult to believe. I also did read about a Messiah or king coming into this world, but I had no idea it was going to be that little man over there.
Virginia	I only believed he was king after Herod killed himself.

Joseph	What are you talking about? Herod dead? No one told us that.
Luke	The strain and stress became too much for him at the palace. He began to lose confidence and finally gave in to the pressures and demands of his wife. He just pulled a dagger and pushed it into his own heart.
Joseph	And now we are free? (Shouts) Mary! Mary! (She answers from inside) Herod is dead. He killed himself. (She runs in with the tray in her hand. She stumbles, tray falls From her hand.)
Luke	Ahh! Just like that! As that tray fell, so did Herod fall, a mighty fall and as the food has scattered, so did the entire palace scatter.
Mary	And there was no one to pick him up, so the food shall remain on the floor. *(Chuckles)*
Joseph	*(bending over)* No, let's get it up, the tray shall rise. This king shall rise.
Martha	Mary, you do have a tremendous responsibility. I will do anything to share your work with you. Let me help you pick the tray up, for I shall help you with this child.
Mary	You will be like my sister, Martha.
Virginia	And I will work too. I shall go all over the country to tell everyone that the infant king is here. Just look at him. *(pointing to Jesus)* He has peace written all over. Let me start with these folk. *(addressing audience)* Jesus is real! Jesus is Real! Believe Him Now! Believe Him Now! He has come to bring peace and joy into this world.
Luke	That's what the prophet said, "How beautiful upon the mountains are the feet of him that *(repeats Isaiah 52:7–10)*

How beautiful on the mountains

are the feet of those who bring good news,

who proclaim peace,

who bring good tidings,

who proclaim salvation,

who say to Zion,

"Your God reigns!"

Listen! Your watchmen lift up their voices;

together they shout for joy.

When the Lord returns to Zion,

they will see it with their own eyes.

Burst into songs of joy together,

you ruins of Jerusalem,

for the Lord has comforted his people,

he has redeemed Jerusalem.

The Lord will lay bare his holy arm

in the sight of all the nations,

and all the ends of the earth will see

the salvation of our God.

Martha	And so, say all of us.
Mary and Joseph	We say the same thing too.
Luke	I have another dream. I am going to be working with the King. I will help to guide him now so that he can help to guide me later. *(noise heard from outside)*
Voice From Outside	This is it. No, it isn't. Of course, it is.
Joseph	Shhh. I'll go to see what this is all about. *(goes to door)*

Luke	There is someone else also who is trying to find the baby Jesus.
Virginia	This news is spreading so fast; I will hardly find anyone left for me to tell. *(TO AUDIENCE)* Maybe all of you out there can go and spread the good news about Jesus Christ.
Mary	I wonder if I'll ever live to see my son grow up and be crowned king. *(Joseph reenters with two men, they are Azor and Perez)*
Joseph	Two men from Herod's palace.
Mary	No, Lord! No! Save us!
Luke	Be wise, gentlemen. This is the Lord's anointed
Joseph	They mean no harm, only good. They too love the king and want to work with him.
Perez	That's why we are here. My name is Perez and I worked in the palace of Herod for years. I told him about his eminent downfall, but he did not believe for he thought it was a joke. I then decided to run away. I have been running since then—running for my life, yet running to find new life. God has answered my prayers for Herod is dead and he was after my life. Now I have found the Christ, I have found new life. *(to audience)* And all you good folk out there can also find New Life in Him
Mary	So he really is dead?
Azor	Yes, he is really dead. I saw him die with my own eyes. My name is Azor and I also worked with Herod. I remember when the news first came to the Palace about the birth of the King. We all laughed at it; it was the joke of the palace, and I shared in the fun.
Virginia	Same story like mine.

Azor	But more and more people kept talking about it and we began to take it more seriously, and finally Herod gave in. He saw defeat coming and so he defeated himself.
Mary	The power of the Lord triumphs over evil.
Azor	And now the whole palace is turned upside- down. My fellow attendants, Obed and Asa, are also searching to find this house and of all the persons who are coming… Tamar, the wife of Herod, is on her way.
Mary	Angels from the realms of glory. Wing your flight o'er all the "earth" he who sang creations story now proclaim Messiah's birth. Come and worship, worship Christ the newborn king.
Virginia	Sages leave your contemplation; brighter visions beam afar. Seek the great desire of nations; we have seen his natal star, come and worship, worship Christ the newborn king.
Joseph	Saints before the altar bending, watching long with hope and fear, suddenly the Lord descending, in his temple shall appear. Come and worship, worship Christ the newborn king. *(all sing chorus twice)*
Narrator/Voice	And as they sang and continued to give thanks there came also as visitors, even Tamar along with Asa and Obed. Joseph invited them in and what a splendid greeting she got.
Tamar	Hail, great one! You shall sit in my place on the throne. There shall be peace and joy in all of the land. *(Mary moves over and hugs her, she sobs for joy. Joseph joins in the triangle and soon all others follow)*
Narrator/Voice:	And that's why we have Christmas. To celebrate the birth of a great king who has brought peace and joy to the world. All over the world the celebration

goes on right through the centuries, the news has been spread and all have joined in the celebration. Songs have been written, stories have been told, but the greatest story ever told was about the birth of a king. The story of A Dream Come True.

A DREAM COME TRUE

List of traditional songs and carols included in musical.

These can be found in most traditional church hymnals or online.

1.   "How Great Thou Art"

2.   "Come Thou Long Expected Jesus. Born to Set Thy People Free"

3.   "Oh, Come, Oh Come Emmanuel.

4.   "See Amid the Winter's Snow"

5.   "O Little Town of Bethlehem" First Two Verses

6.   "Angels from the Realms of Glory" First Verse and Chorus

7.   "All Glory Laud and Honor" First Two Verses

8.   "Sing we the King who is coming to reign

About the Author

The Rev. Dr. Errol E Leslie is the founding pastor of Grace and Mercy Ministries Inc. Palm Bay, Florida. Prior to starting that congregation, he served as a pastor in the Methodist Church of the Caribbean and the Americas, as well as the Florida and the New England Conferences of the United Methodist Church.

He is originally from Jamaica where he attended high school, college, and seminary. In high school, he was very involved in the interschool Christian fellowships and participated in several weekend residential camps, all of which turned out to be spiritually uplifting.

After graduating seminary, he served a number of small churches where he specialized in evangelism and youth ministry to include being a camp counsellor for several years in the Methodist church.

He previously published the book Stolen Grace in which he tells the story of his journey in and departure from the United Methodist Church. Although not having any professional training in theater, Rev. Dr.

Leslie has used his innate talent throughout the years to utilize drama as a very useful and effective tool throughout his ministry.

His love for and involvement in drama started from his days in high school when he would work backstage during productions as well as playing various roles onstage including several lead roles. During this same period as a teenager, he would write, direct, and produce Christian plays which were done competitively at church events. He also wrote plays which did not necessarily carry a Christian theme, but still earned rave reviews in the communities in which they would be performed.

His passion for the arts continued during his college and seminary days as once more, he would play leading roles in plays at that level. His first opportunity to perform internationally came in 1976 when he visited Nassau in the Bahamas for a series of concerts. He then participated in both drama and music as he was also a member of the UTCWI (United Theological College of the West Indies) singers.

Rev. Dr. Leslie is also a singer and a self-taught musician with the gift of being able to play several musical instruments. For a long time, he and his family participated in a reggae gospel music ministry where they were able to minster in song to several audiences all over Jamaica and in several states within the USA.

He is happy to share these two musicals with the rest of the world, with the hope that there will be several more Bible-based musicals to follow.

The Lord He Made Us

Text: ERROL LESLIE   Music: ERROL LESLIE

A King Is Born (F)

Text: ERROL LESLIE

Music: ERROL LESLIE

A King Is Born (Eb)

Text: ERROL LESLIE   Music: ERROL LESLIE

What News Is this

Text: ERROL LESLIE

TRADITIONAL
Arrangement: ERROL LESLIE

To Egypt We Go

Text: ERROL LESLIE

Music: ERROL LESLIE